DIPLODOCUS

by Janet Riehecky
illustrated by Jim Conaway

THE CHILD'S WORLD

MANKATO, MN

Grateful appreciation is expressed to
Bret S. Beall, Research Consultant,
Field Museum of Natural History, Chicago,
Illinois, who reviewed this book to
insure its accuracy.

Library of Congress Cataloging in Publication Data

Riehecky, Janet, 1953-
  Diplodocus / by Janet Riehecky ; illustrated by Jim Conaway.
    p. cm. — (Dinosaur books)
  Summary: Presents facts and speculations about the physical
characteristics and behavior of this long-necked herbivorous dinosaur.
  ISBN 0-89565-627-2
  1. Diplodocus—Juvenile literature. [1. Diplodocus.
2. Dinosaurs.] I. Conaway, James, 1944-   ill. II. Title.
III. Series: Riehecky, Janet, 1953-   Dinosaur books.
QE862.S3R535   1990
567.9'7—dc20   90-42520
                                                         CIP
                                                          AC

DIPLODOCUS

When people think of dinosaurs, one word they often think of is *long*!

Dinosaurs lived a *long* time ago, and they lived on the earth for a *long* time. But the longest thing about dinosaurs was the dinosaurs themselves.

Some dinosaurs had long teeth.

And some had long horns.

There were dinosaurs that had long legs . . .

8

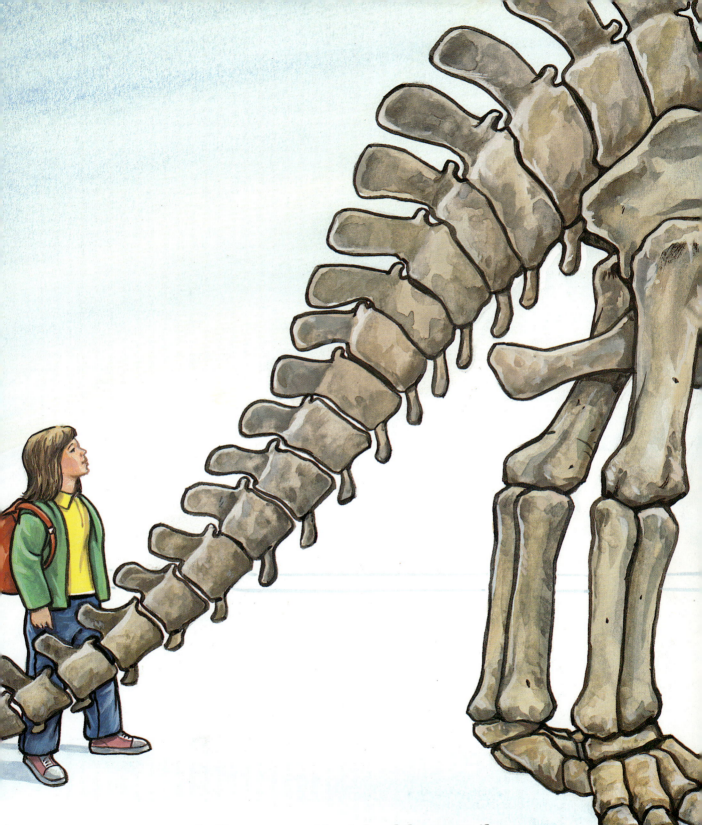

and dinosaurs that had long tails.

But one type of dinosaur really gave new meaning to the word "long." It was the Diplodocus (di-PLOD-uh-kuss). The name Diplodocus means "double beam." A beam is a long piece of wood or metal that is often used to support a floor or ceiling. The Diplodocus had not one but two "beams" of bone supporting and protecting its long tail. It needed an extra "beam" because the Diplodocus was one of the longest dinosaurs that ever lived.

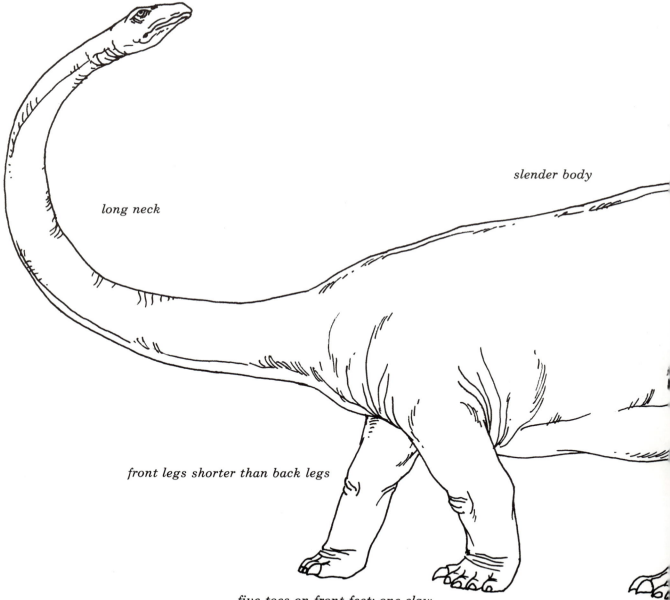

small head

long neck

slender body

front legs shorter than back legs

five toes on front feet; one claw

The largest Diplodocus was about ninety feet from the tip of its tail to the end of its nose. That's almost as long as a basketball court. (How would you like to have a creature that long on your team!) Most of its length was neck (twenty-six feet) and tail (forty-six feet). Its body was actually quite slender compared to its relatives. Its body was "only" thirteen feet tall at the hips and weighed "only" ten or eleven tons. That's as large as three or four elephants, which is enormous compared to you or me, but not compared to many other dinosaurs.

whiplike tail

five toes on back feet; three claws

On top of its very long neck, Diplodocus had a small head, with a very small brain. This huge creature had a brain about the size of a kitten's brain. Most scientists think this meant it wasn't a very smart dinosaur. Its brain wasn't even big enough to control all the movements of its body. It had a nerve center in its hips to handle the back legs and tail.

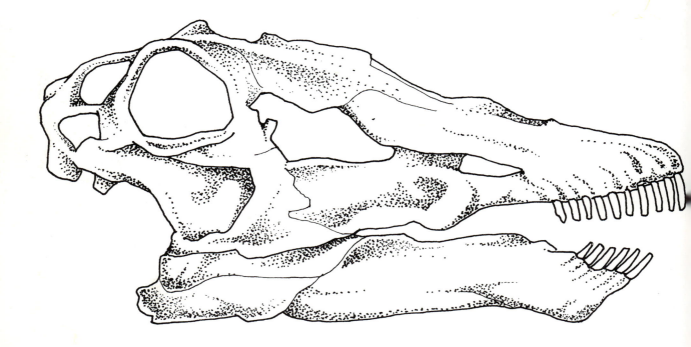

Diplodocus may not have been too long on brains, but it was smart enough to know what to do if it saw a meat-eating dinosaur—RUN! But Diplodocus wasn't built for a lot of speed, so sometimes it had to fight.

The best defense the Diplodocus had was its long tail. It could use its tail as a whip, lashing at a meat eater. Even the fierce Allosaurus could be knocked down by a blow from that tail.

If a meat eater stayed away from the tail by attacking from the front, the Diplodocus might still be able to defend itself. It could slash at the attacker with a sharp claw it had on each front foot. Or it could rear up on its back legs and try to crush the attacker with its huge front legs. But even though these were good defenses, they were not enough if the Diplodocus was attacked by a pack of meat eaters.

To avoid this, the Diplodocus may have stayed in herds most of the time. The little dinosaurs would be kept in the center of the herd where meat eaters couldn't get to them. Most meat eaters, seeing a large number of huge beasts, would look for smaller, easier prey.

It's hard to imagine one huge Diplodocus, but think about a herd of twenty or thirty. They would have covered an area larger than the biggest football stadium—and they would have been eating every plant in sight!

A Diplodocus needed to eat lots and lots of food. In fact, it didn't even bother to take time to chew. It just stripped the leaves off a tree, swallowed, and went back for another mouthful. Every now and then it would swallow a few rocks to help break up the food in its stomach. After it ate all the leaves that were low on a tree, it would rear up on its back legs to reach the tender leaves higher up. After all, it wouldn't want to leave anything uneaten.

Occasionally the Diplodocus might have taken time off from eating to go for a swim. Scientists have found footprints they think are from a swimming Diplodocus. The footprints show the Diplodocus let most of its body float in the water. It pushed itself along by pushing off the bottom of the lake with just its two front feet. (The hippopotamus of today swims the same way.) When the Diplodocus wanted to turn left or right, it put its back legs or tail on the bottom and pushed in the direction it wanted to go. Imagine the splash a creature that size could make!

Scientists have studied the footprints and bones of the Diplodocus, and these have told us a lot about this dinosaur. But there are still many things we don't know.

For instance, we will probably never know what color the Diplodocus was. Even if scientists should find skin that is fossilized, the millions of passing years would have changed its color, most likely leaving it grey or brown. For all we know, the Diplodocus could have been bright red with yellow polka-dots!

Also, scientists have not found any of the soft parts of the Diplodocus' body. We don't know whether it had big ears, little ears, or no ears, or whether it had any loose flaps of skin. Some scientists have argued that Diplodocus might have had a trunk. The Diplodocus' nose is very high up between its eyes. Animals of today that have that kind of nose, such as elephants and tapirs, also have trunks.

So maybe the Diplodocus did have a trunk — or maybe not. Most scientists think it wouldn't have had any need for one because it had such a long neck.

We will probably never know for sure what color the Diplodocus was or whether or not it had a trunk. There will always be things we don't know about this long dinosaur—even if we study it for a long, long time!

Dinosaur Fun

Scientists can discover a lot about a dinosaur by studying its footprints. To make it easier to study the prints, scientists sometimes make a plaster cast of them.

You can pretend you are a scientist and make a plaster print of an animal's footprints. You will need:

— plaster of Paris (and a can to mix it in)
— water
— a strip of heavy paper about 4 inches by 12 inches
— tape

1. First, look for an animal's footprints in hardened mud or sand. You may find prints from a rabbit, bird, or even your dog!
2. When you find some prints, make a ring out of the strip of paper and tape it closed. Put the ring around the print and gently press it into the mud or sand.
3. Mix the plaster, using a little more water than the directions call for to make the plaster a little thinner. Pour the plaster over the print.
4. Let the plaster dry completely. Then remove it from the print to see what you find!

398